LADIES LEGACIES

ESTATE PLANNING FOR WOMEN

KELLY LONGTIN, ESQ.

FOUNDER OF KELLY LONGTIN LAW, PLLC

Jacobs & Whitehall
21750 Hardy Oak Blvd
Suite 104 – 51700
San Antonio, Texas 78258
(888) 570-7338
www.jacobsandwhitehall.com

Ordering Information:

Quantity sales. Special discounts are available on quantity purchases by corporations, associations, and others. For details, contact the publisher at the address above.

Orders by U.S. trade bookstores and wholesalers. Please contact Jacobs & Whitehall: Tel: (888) 991-2766 or visit www.jacobsandwhitehall.com.

Printed in the United States of America

Published in 2022

ISBN: 978-1-954506-38-1

PREFACE

In the beginning of my career as an estate planning attorney, I met with a client who unknowingly changed my life. This client's husband had just passed away; she was scared – almost frantic – when I met with her. She and her husband had been married for a very long time and he had always managed the finances; here she was now, alone and having to navigate not only the emotional death of her husband, but the rest of her life without him in it. She didn't know which banks held their money, what bills needed to be paid, or even how much money she had to pay them. As an attorney with her as my client, this experience was heartbreaking. But it was this woman's fear – her jolting realization that she was completely out of the "financial" loop – that motivated me to do whatever I could to help women be prepared in situations like these. In fact, I even made a promise to myself: from that point forward, I would do whatever it takes to educate and empower women, one lady at a time.

I have spent my entire legal career practicing and focusing solely on Estate Planning. I have had the honor of helping thousands of families plan their estates and I am happy to share my experience and knowledge with you to help you plan for yours. While you will learn a lot as you read this book, there is no substitute for working with a qualified estate planning attorney, and other financial professionals to ensure you plan well and leave a legacy you can be proud of.

I truly love working with families and helping them navigate the difficult choices that must be made to put their estate plan in place and providing them with peace of mind knowing that their families will be well taken care of.

For your benefit, I have provided an appendix at the end of the book. It contains the Ladies Legacies™ workbook and guide to help you with your estate planning and with your finances. I want to welcome you as a member of the Ladies Legacies family and congratulate you for taking one step further to making sure you leave a lasting legacy behind.

DEDICATION

"Just when the caterpillar thought it was going to die, it became a beautiful butterfly."

— Unknown

This book is dedicated to the ladies in the world who work and strive every day to protect and provide for their loved ones. Sometimes we just don't know the best way to do this. It is my hope that after reading this book, you walk away with an understanding of how to provide for and protect your loved ones, even when you are physically or mentally unable to. I aim to give you the strength to deal with some of life's most difficult topics, like death and incapacity. We never know how strong we are until we must be. I know that the passion to do what is best for yourself and your loved ones sits firmly inside of you, as the same passion does in me. I am simply here to guide you along the way. Be strong, be fierce, and leave the legacy that you want.

ACKNOWLEDGEMENT

I would like to take this opportunity to thank my parents, my children, my family, my friends, my clients, my paralegal, and all of those who have crossed my path.

Thank you to:

My father and his wife for giving me a loving home, for being patient as I tested out my independence, and for not smothering my free spirit.

My mother, my friend, for showing me that one can overcome anything in life. Your strength is beautiful, and I thank you for showing it to me.

My other dad, Elliott. Thank you for believing in me and for giving me the wings to fly. Thank you for all of our conversations about how to make a bigger dent in life, while always being kind and respectful to people.

My family for setting high standards for being a good person in life. I strive every day to exceed those standards.

My children, Skylah and Alexis, who have taught me the meaning of unconditional love. You are my strength, my motivation, and the reason I feel like I can conquer the world. You both have grown into tremendously kind and giving ladies, and I cannot wait to see what else my butterflies become. Thank you for your patience and understanding as I focused on my career and my personal growth. I strive every day to be a good role model for you and to help women gain the strength that the two of you give me.

My friends, for always accepting me, and for the endless, hearty laughs we share. Thank you for showing me what is truly important in life.

My paralegal, Pennie. Thank you for taking a leap of faith, and for always having my back. You have made this leg of the journey so enjoyable. I look forward to many more adventures together.

To my clients, thank you for allowing me to be such an integral part of your life and for putting your confidence in me to develop a plan to protect and provide for your family. Thank you for telling your friends and family about the Kelly Longtin Law family, and for encouraging them to become members as well.

And to all the people who I encounter daily. I believe you learn something from everyone who crosses your path. From that first client who unknowingly ignited my desire to develop the Ladies Legacies focus, to the wonderful cashier at the grocery store; I thank you for the impact you have on my thoughts and my life journey, and I look forward to the changes you all bring about in me.

Lastly, but perhaps most importantly, I thank all of the ladies who are reading this book. I thank you for your desire to learn and grow, your courage to be uncomfortable as you plan for your potential incapacity and inevitable death, and your wisdom in knowing that tackling these tough topics is something that just can't wait any longer.

DISCLAIMER

This publication is intended to be used for educational purposes only. No legal advice is being given, and no attorney-client relationship is intended to be created by reading this material. The author assumes no liability for any errors or omissions or for how this book or its contents are used to interpret or for any consequences resulting directly or indirectly from the use of this book. For legal or any other advice, please consult an experienced attorney or the appropriate expert who is aware of the specific facts of your case and is knowledgeable of the law in your jurisdiction.

Kelly Longtin Law, PLLC

565 Turnpike Street
Suite 65
North Andover, MA 01845
www.kellylongtinlaw.com
MA (978) 566-3500
NH (603) 506-4817
Licensed in Massachusetts and New Hampshire

TESTIMONIALS

"Kelly has been my guiding light through these last few years. I am so grateful for her professional, brilliant, attentive, considerate, honest and most of all caring way she has conducted me through my mother's death, my trust and guidance and patience. I am thankful for her support. I feel like Kelly is family and I have referred friends to her. I carry Kelly's cards in my purse. Pennie was also an important part in updating and contacting me numerous times. I can't thank these women enough for their impressive help. All my ducks are in a row now." – **Joanne Kun**

****

"It took me about a year and a half to find a good law firm that I could build rapport with and feel comfortable to communicate what I wanted in my trust. I have zero experience with writing a trust or a will, I only had an idea of what I wanted in a trust but could not figure out how I could even word it. I came across other attorneys charging higher fees, but they only provided half the services that Attorney Kelly Longtin provided. I felt comfortable telling

10

her my goals and she was able to put all my requests into a trust and answer all of my questions." – **KG**

****

"I felt immediately comfortable with Kelly and her team. Truly professional, knowledgeable and genuinely kind and helpful with all the questions I had. I know that any questions or concerns I would have, I can just make a call. I know people always say there is always room for improvement, but I honestly cannot think of any. I love them!" – **Rosemary Carter Molnar**

****

"Kelly is a top-notch attorney for estate planning. I found her a couple years ago (after lots of atty research), and I'm so glad I did! She asks questions other attorneys never ask about your life, family, future, nursing home care, LTC, etc. and she prepares the documents with that plan, and the future, in mind. When she's done, she's not like other attys who you'll never see again, you'll have a relationship with Kelly that will last a lifetime. She's clear, concise and VERY thorough in all aspects of what needs to be done. She's gone way beyond what our other atty did for our estate plan to make sure our monies are safe for us and our children. We can't speak enough about what Kelly

can offer in person, by phone or by text. She's very responsive and always willing to help out where needed! My husband and I HIGHLY RECOMMEND Kelly Longtin for Estate Planning (and we're picky)!!" — **Karen & Steven Roy**

****

"Kelly and Pennie are professionals every step of the planning process. It's not always easy dealing with end of life decisions, however, Kelly helps you every step of the way in a manner most pleasant, at least for me. Go see Kelly as soon as you can!" — **MRM**

****

"My husband and I recently decided to have a Revocable Trust done. Attorney Longtin came highly recommended. We made an appointment to meet with her and her team. Not knowing much about the process of estate planning, we were a bit uneasy and did not know where to begin. Attorney Longtin and her team put us at ease and held our hand explaining our options and answering our many questions every step of the way. During the process many confidential and personal things need to be discussed in order to make intelligent decisions. Attorney Longtin provided the level of care and concern that made us

*feel extremely comfortable. Well after everything was set Attorney Longtin was available for prompt replies to any additional questions and concerns we had. If you have not set up your trust yet, make an appointment with Attorney Kelly Longtin." – **Sharon & John Inza**

****

*"Kelly Longtin Law's services are exceptional. All of our concerns were addressed professionally and in a timely manner. They were extremely flexible with rescheduling appointments. We appreciate all of their help." – **Charles & Claire**

****

"My daughter and I had to make a decision to find an attorney after the death of my husband. My husband and I procrastinated about getting our estate plan together – BIG MISTAKE! With the help of my daughter and a good friend, Kelly Longtin came highly recommended. We made our appointment and the day we went to her office we were warmly greeted by her assistant Pennie who seated us. Within five minutes we met Kelly, no waiting, right on time. Within minutes, she made both my daughter and myself very comfortable. Listening to our issues, she showed compassion and kindness. She took extra effort

explaining certain things about the law that we did not know or understand. She assured us we could contact her at any time, which we did. All that weight was taken off my shoulders. She did a great job. I'm glad I met Kelly Longtin." — **Rose G.**

****

"Attorney Kelly Longtin and her team have made this experience as smooth as possible. I had a lot of questions and each was answered courteously and quickly. The organization and knowledge was outstanding. I appreciate the work they have done for me and my family." — **A Raving Fan**

****

"Kelly is the utmost professional along with being respectful, honest in her advice, reliable and so very approachable. We felt as though she were part of the family after leaving her office. We had quite a bit going on with our properties and business and Kelly made sense of all of it! No easy feat to say the least. We will recommend Kelly highly to our family and friends. We feel this will most certainly be a long relationship!" — **JB & JB**

****

"Kelly was referred to us by a family member and we are glad he did. Kelly was very helpful in getting our Estate Planning *together and answered any questions we had. Kelly also made sure we understood what she was saying. Kelly made sure we covered all our bases from A to Z. Kelly is very friendly and made us feel at ease. I found Kelly to be very knowledgeable at her job, and if we had any questions about our plan to let her know. Kelly treats you more than just a customer, you are more like a good friend or family member and I would highly recommend her services to anyone."* — **Mark W.**

****

"Would recommend Kelly Longtin law to everyone!" — **SAW**

****

"I was anxious walking into the office. Another thing to check off my bucket list. Pennie greeted me professional, kind and warm – so was the coffee. Kelly was more interested in my life than what I was there for until I realized she needed all the information to put me in the best plan for me. She is so knowledgeable and patient with me. I felt good leaving with a clear mind and understanding all pieces of the trust. Thank you ladies!" — **Karen McKim**

****

"As first time customers we were very satisfied with the clarity and timeliness with the estate planning process. The communication was efficient and the tools used to exchange information were effective. The end product, our estate plan was very satisfying." – **Mark & Lisa Tardiff**

****

"Kelly was so helpful and made a very scary experience easy and manageable! What made our experience even more valuable was her friendly and open approach. So grateful to have her guidance!" – **Roger & Stephanie Power**

****

"I wanted to update a Trust. The two meetings with Attorney Longtin before the signing were professional and with good communication via Zoom calls, emails and reminder phone calls. She listened to my concerns and made good suggestions. At the signing, I was impressed with the detailed explanations of options and answering of questions. The Trust and other documents were well organized in a notebook. It was a great experience." – **NK**

****

"Kelly was very pleasant to deal with at all times. She explained things in layman's terms so I would understand completely. Kelly was accessible when necessary to me and my family. I found her extremely knowledgeable regarding this matter. She also was very sensitive to my needs and wants. I would highly recommend her as an estate planning attorney." – **Janice Kalp**

****

"Excellent – 5 STAR – friendly, professional and very helpful. Kelly thought of every need that may rise. I would recommend Kelly to anyone." – **JC**

****

"I very proudly endorse Kelly Longtin, she is always one of my most trusted resources, both personally and professionally. Kelly always shows that she not only cares deeply about her clients' legal cases, but also about their personal lives and their families. Her drive and work ethics are second to none and I would not hesitate to recommend her to anyone in need of legal services." – **Attorney David Haughton**

****

"Professionalism at its finest! Kelly & Pennie are wonderfully accessible. They are so knowledgeable with putting a trust together. Such a great experience dealing with them both. They made a difficult subject easy to deal with." — **Shaun and Sallie Moynihan**

****

"Kelly explained everything to the fullest and I was very confident in her abilities. Kelly was very organized and thorough and I feel very secure with all she has done for me. I recommend her to do all of your estate planning." — **Jennifer Hartman**

****

"Kelly is professional, organized, and extremely efficient. She helped me personally as well as my family for matters big and small and left me feeling confident and secure. I will be recommending Kelly to anyone I know in need of the services she offers!" — **Jacquelyn Censullo**

****

"Kelly is the most honest professional attorney. I have used Kelly's services for my trust and my family utilizes her as well. I

would highly recommend her to my clients and many of them have used her services and were very satisfied." — **Connie Doto**

****

"Everything was quick, easy and efficient. Kelly is wonderful and kind. She put me right at ease. Her staff is friendly and fun! For estate planning they are the best. Thank you Kelly and staff! — **Marie A. Guay**

****

"This was an extremely easy and comprehensive process. I feel a great sense of relief having this taken care of. The end product is particularly easy to understand and utilize." — **SW**

****

"Absolutely love the way Kelly conducts her business! She and Pennie made me totally comfortable doing my trust, etc. Kelly is so knowledgeable and explained everything in a way I could understand – Love her!" — **Bev Maxwell**

****

"Kelly made the process of getting my will together simple. She always had my best interests in mind as we discussed and reviewed. She is a pleasure to work with. Highly recommend!" – **Heidi J. Schluter**

****

"Kelly was extremely knowledgeable and helpful through the whole process. She explained everything very carefully and answered any questions we had. I would highly recommend her services." – **Claire Piccirillo**

****

"Kelly was very easy to work with and explained everything in detail! Thank you for going above and beyond! Your knowledge is much appreciated." – **Elizabeth & Peter Bata**

****

"I find Kelly highly knowledgeable in the law. She took great care to make the process smooth. She was exceptional and comforting during the process and I would recommend her to anyone!" – **DMB**

****

"I am completely satisfied with Kelly's professionalism, knowledge and dedication to her practice. I felt and feel very comfortable working on my affairs with Kelly." — **Cathy Z.**

****

"It was a pleasure meeting with Kelly in planning my estate package. Her expertise was so valuable in all aspects of organizing my estate, it brought me much comfort and peace of mind." — **MMJ**

****

"Friendly, courteous service with the client's interest at heart. Professional knowledge of all aspects of estate planning." — **Phil Askew**

****

"Kelly is a quintessential professional! Typically doing a trust is an emotional and very difficult process. Kelly made it an absolute joyful experience." — **Deirdre Houtmeyers**

****

"Efficient client service. Pleasant and responsive staff. Very knowledgeable and explained everything in simple terms." — **KJ**

****

"Very efficient. Easy to understand and felt comfortable with choices and my wishes." — **Alexandria Christmas**

****

"Kelly has been most helpful, and I am so pleased my Financial Advisor referred me to Kelly." — **PES**

****

"Quick response time, very approachable, and easy to communicate with!" — **James & Rebecca Toomey**

****

"Kelly is extremely knowledgeable and has a great way of explaining these very impactful life decisions." — **PPC**

****

Thank you to all my clients for their kind words. It is truly my privilege to be entrusted with your estate planning needs. — **Kelly**

TABLE OF CONTENTS

ABOUT THE AUTHOR

I want to begin by sharing with you why I am so passionate about helping LADIES plan for the future and the future of their families, and about guiding them through the process of leaving behind their legacies. When I speak about "legacies," I am not just referring to the monetary legacy one leaves behind to their heirs, but also to the memories, values, and stories they pass along.

For as long as I can remember, it has been a desire and focus of mine to help women become successful in life. Maybe this desire took hold when I was a child, as I was always taught by my parents that I could do anything I wanted in life, as long as I put my mind to it. Or maybe it was being the only female in my family — surrounded by a sea of males — that spurred this thought process and the passionate focus it led to.

As an adolescent, this desire grew even stronger. I would find myself standing up for my rights against school administrators for being treated differently from the boys. Why did I have to take off my fashionable hat when the boys were routinely allowed to wear baseball hats — forwards or backwards or any which way they preferred?

In retrospect, it seems odd that such a seemingly inconsequential incident would make such a significant and lasting impact on my life, but it did. In fact, I believe that one request — to remove my hat when the boys could leave theirs on — and the feeling of injustice it stirred in me has become a guiding force in my quest to represent women of all demographics in the estate planning process, and to help women flourish in this game we call life.

As I gained more life experience, my knowledge and self-confidence grew steadily, right along with my motivation to encourage and assist women in becoming more present in their own lives and futures. This became the overarching goal of my work with women, whether that work revolved around addressing estate planning needs to protect their families, or coaching women to become healthier in their mind, body, and soul.

People often ask me why I chose to focus exclusively on estate planning, and my answer always brings me back to the reason I chose to become an attorney in the first place: I really wanted to help people, whether they were male or female, young or old, single or married. I have always had a love for people and their stories—stories of triumph and failure and all of the things that guide people through the journey of life.

As a child, I spent every day with my grandparents, listening to the stories that not only defined them, but reflected their love for their family. I believe it was the bond with my grandparents that initially pulled me into the world of estate planning, where I could work with people—mostly older couples—who loved their families just as much as my grandparents loved theirs. I realized that I could give these people peace of mind in knowing that when they are no longer here, their loved ones will be protected and cared for. Estate planning just felt like a natural fit for me.

I remember the day I became acutely aware that I needed to use my gift and education more specifically— to further help ladies in life. It started with a single call from an estate planning client. As we sat down, this woman told me that her husband had just passed away, and what followed was an unprecedented pouring of emotion—so much so that it was almost palpable. I can still remember the look of fear on her face, and the sound of it in her voice as she explained that since her husband had always handled the finances, she didn't even know how to access their money.

I made a promise to her and myself that day that I would help prevent other women from finding themselves in the same position. To that end, I designed an event called "What To Do When Your Husband Dies," which focused specifically on this issue.

Over time, I expanded this notion of helping women in all different demographics and situations ... and Ladies Legacies was born.

I am now an experienced speaker on women's issues and estate planning, and I frequently present Ladies Legacies webinars to educate women on life and estate planning. I continue to grow my presence in the ever-changing social media space via podcasts, YouTube, Facebook, and Instagram—so be sure to follow Kelly Longtin Law (@kellytlaw).

Why Write a Book?

My goal in writing this book is to educate women in all phases of life about the importance of estate planning, to help them recognize the unique issues that apply to their particular demographic, and to encourage them to be assertive in all facets of life.

This book is meant for women of all ages and situations, including millennials, single women, women who choose not to marry, women in traditional marriages, women in same-sex marriages, divorced women, young mothers with young children, middle-aged women with teenagers, and older women with children who have grown and left the nest.

Wait... What the Heck is Estate Planning, Exactly?

Estate planning is a lot like life itself; it continues to change and evolve over time. But what never changes is the absolute need for a woman to have an estate plan in place that meets her needs and goals, and since those will change over the course of her life, so too will her estate plan. This is why it's so important for women to have an estate planning attorney whom they trust to be there at each and every stage of their life.

An 'estate' is simply everything that a person owns, including their home and any other real estate, bank accounts, investments and brokerage accounts, retirement benefits, life insurance proceeds, and personal belongings.

Estate planning is the process by which a legal plan is created to ensure that what a person wants to have happen after their incapacitation or death – in terms of their estate, financial decisions, and health care decisions—indeed happens. This written plan allows a person to control who will receive their assets and property when they die, and how they will receive it. This plan can also ensure that less money is paid to Uncle Sam in taxes, and that more money is available for the family.

It's important to reiterate that estate planning is not only about what happens when a person dies, but about what happens to that person should they become incapacitated. The right estate plan will let the creator of it (as opposed to the courts) maintain control of their assets, financial decisions, and health care decisions. It will also allow the creator to protect some or all of their assets when an incapacity arises.

Some women believe that their family members— for the simple fact that they are "family"—will automatically be able to handle these matters for them, but without a written estate plan in place, it is actually the courts that will be handling and overseeing these matters.

CHAPTER 1

LISTEN UP, LADIES!

What every woman needs to know to protect themselves, their money, and their family.

Estate planning issues affect women more profoundly than men.

Why? Because women are most likely to have the final say when it comes down to passing on the family's wealth. There are many reasons for this, such as:

- Women outlive men

- Women inherit from both their spouses and their parents
- Divorce occurs in over 50% of marriages
- Women are choosing not to marry at all
- Women are occupying a larger percentage of the workforce
- Women are entering careers with higher-paying salaries
- More women own businesses now than ever before (and I predict this number will continue to grow ☺)

While there may not be substantial differences in planning for men and women, there is no question that women approach things differently when it comes to life, and therefore when it comes to estate planning. For example, women are more likely to talk through issues and generally have a greater need to feel listened to and heard, which is why they want to work with someone who not only understands their concerns, but can address those concerns in the context of their philosophy of life.

Most women have estate planning goals that center around the family. They want to protect their children and ensure an easy transition of assets to their children, and almost always want to keep the courts out of the process. They also want to do what they can to ensure that family harmony will be maintained when they are no longer around to be the peacekeeper, and worry about how their death might impact the family dynamics or disturb the relationships between their children and grandchildren.

Concerns surrounding incapacitation are also common. I often hear women voice their concerns about the financial and emotional burden that could fall on their children should they become incapacitated, especially if their children are left to become their caretakers.

When women fail to plan, their main concerns will most certainly not be met, and they will subject their families to the very issues that they so desperately want to avoid. Instead of harnessing the power and ability to be in control of their health care decisions and financial decisions — including where their money will go when they pass—they will be subjecting their children to endless court procedures and ultimately leaving all of these decisions in the hands of a judge wearing a black robe.

Can you imagine if we lived our daily lives with absolutely no say about how they go or what happens? Probably not. So, why are so many women okay with having no input on matters of their life, death, and legacy?

Why Every Woman Needs an Estate Plan— Let's Break It Down:

1. Financial security. A woman must plan her estate not only to ensure her own financial security and that of her children or other family members, but also to ensure the proper distribution of her assets to her family, friends, and charitable organizations.

2. To plan for her spouse's entrance into a nursing home. Statistically, men die or become incapacitated much sooner than women, which makes it particularly important for married women to protect their assets by planning for the possibility that their

spouse will become incapacitated and need long term care in a nursing home.

In the absence of proper planning, all of the joint assets between the woman and her incapacitated spouse will have to be used to pay for the incapacitated spouse's stay in a nursing home, which is around $168,000 per year in Massachusetts and New Hampshire. It's clear that this can quickly push women and their families into bankruptcy. For this reason, it's critical for women to consider whether they will have enough money to live comfortably should their spouse become incapacitated.

3. To plan for the possibility of her own incapacitation. Women in all demographics need to plan for the possibility of their own incapacity. Women don't always look at the financial fallout of their own incapacitation, but instead tend to focus on emotional factors, such as who will take care of them, and who will take care of the people who they are taking care of, such as their parents, an aging spouse, or even grandchildren (over three million grandparents are currently raising their grandchildren, and this number continues to grow).

Many women also have a fear of their children fighting or disagreeing over their care. Some women worry about being alone and not having anyone there to care for them, which is a real possibility as the number of women who never marry is rising, and because women statistically outlive their male partners.

4. Control. By putting a plan in place, a woman will have control over her affairs while she is alive and after she passes away. This includes control over medical decisions in the event that she becomes unable to express those decisions herself due to incapacitation. It also includes control over who will handle her finances (and will prevent these decisions from being made by a judge).

Creating an estate plan will also allow a woman to determine which family members will inherit her assets after she passes away. This is especially important for women who are in a second marriage and want to make sure that their children are not accidentally disinherited, and also that they themselves are not accidentally disinherited in the event that their spouse passes before they do.

5. To appoint a guardian for minor children. A priority for women with minor children is to create an estate plan that appoints a specific guardian who will care for her minor children in the event that they pass away or become incapacitated and unable to care for their children themselves. By failing to create an estate plan and putting her wishes on paper, a mother relinquishes control to the courts, which will decide who to appoint as guardian of her minor children. Contrary to what most people think, the court will not always choose a family member, and may even appoint a total stranger.

6. Business protection. Any woman who has her own business needs to protect her family from the significant amount of work that could be created should she pass away or become incapacitated without having made a plan for what will happen to her business.

7. Court avoidance. To make things as easy as possible for her loved ones, a woman needs to provide a written plan for dealing with her affairs and estate. This will prevent family members from having to

endure complicated court procedures. While there will always be some administrative work to deal with following the death of a family member, having an estate plan in place will ensure that the process is as simple and streamlined as possible for the beneficiaries. In turn, this will have the benefit of reducing anxiety and frustration in an already emotional and difficult time for those loved ones.

8.   Greater need for financial resources. There is a greater need for women to plan because they will have a greater need for financial resources. Whether or not it's for biological reasons, numbers don't lie: the average life span for a female is five years longer than that of our male counterparts. On average, 71% of people in nursing homes are women, which is not new statistical information. The facts clearly show that women have always had a longer expected lifespan than men, and it is time to stop ignoring this.

Women, Societal Changes, and Estate Planning

Are women creating a new age of women and wealth? Although the equal pay gap still exists, women are redefining wealth in this country. It is hard to believe that women who were predominately stay-at-home mothers and housewives fifty years ago now make up half of the work force in this country. This staggering increase has led to a new age of women and wealth. As of 2021, women held over $72 trillion, which means they hold over 32% of the wealth in this country.

These percentages are expected to continue to grow ... but why? There are several contributing factors:

#1 — Millennials. Millennial women are changing the way women are viewed, and are also having a tremendous impact on the world and the financial state of women. Millennials might even be breaking the seemingly antiquated thoughts that men should be the breadwinners for families. As of 2021, 72% of millennial women were in the workforce and are showing no fear, with over 28% of these women choosing to start their own businesses. I think it is safe to say that we are about to see a new launching of women and wealth.

#2 — The choice to forgo marriage. Another contributing factor is that more and more women are choosing not to marry. This is allowing women to single-handedly accumulate wealth in their name, adding to the already trillions of dollars women own.

#3 — The rising divorce rate in the United States. This is having a definite effect on the wealth dichotomy in this country. With half of marriages ending in divorce, women are becoming financially responsible and independent. Due to the circumstances of life, women are being forced to learn how to invest and plan for their own futures and those of their loved ones.

#4 — Women continue to outlive men. The fact that women statistically outlive men is having a profound effect on the increase of women's wealth in the United States, and it means that women have to plan for the passing of assets to loved ones. When all of the money is transferred from the husband to the wife, it doubles the value of the woman's estate and changes the amount of wealth women hold. This is not the only time that women will inherit wealth during their lifetime;

keep in mind that women will most likely inherit from their parents as well, further adding to the pool of wealth for which women are increasingly responsible.

#5 — Evolving beliefs. Over the last few generations, there's been a change in women's beliefs — changes that have allowed women to pursue education and careers that they may not have previously considered. More and more, women are becoming entrepreneurs and breaking the glass ceilings in higher-paying professions (e.g., physician, lawyer, business executive). With more women focusing on careers and becoming financial role models for the youth, it will be interesting to see just how fast women will equalize the wealth in this country.

Given all of these factors, women will be left to manage all of their wealth — whether it's been earned or inherited. They will also be responsible for making final decisions about how things are invested and how money is spent or saved for their beneficiaries. Although men may have started out in this role, with the majority of people over the age of 75 being women and with women having more wealth, it is clear that this responsibility will ultimately fall to the female population. For this reason, women need to be educated about the importance of proper planning, and feel comfortable working with the professionals who can help them.

CHAPTER 2

ESTATE PLANNING STRATEGIES FOR THE MS., MISS, AND MRS.

What Almost Every Lady's Estate Plan Needs (and Why!)

There are some key estate planning documents that are essential to every effective estate plan, and every woman should know what these documents are, how they work, and whether or not they need them.

It's no secret that in the legal field, we tend to use different names to describe the same documents, just to keep everyone guessing and to add to the confusion (I will do my best to clarify this as we go along).

☐ Financial power of attorney. What is it, how does it work, and who really needs one? A financial power of attorney, also called a durable power of attorney, is a legal document that allows a person to choose whom they would like to take over legal authority to deal with their finances (e.g., bank accounts, retirement accounts, deeds, etc.). This very important document is only valid when you are alive, and will cease to have any legal authority once you pass away.

If you suddenly became incapacitated – today – who would legally be able to manage your finances for you? Who would be able to write checks on your behalf in order to pay for your mortgage and other bills? Answering these types of questions is essential to executing the ever so important financial power of attorney document.

Most women have not really thought about it, or incorrectly assume that a family member would be able to just step in and handle these affairs. They assume that if they are married or have children, their spouse and/or children would automatically be allowed to take care of these matters.

THIS IS NOT TRUE! If a person has not given someone the legal authority to act on their behalf when it comes to financial matters, and if that person becomes unable to handle their affairs due to an illness or an incapacity, then their family members will have to go to court to be appointed conservator. The conservator will have the ability to deal with a person's financial matters, but every transaction will be overseen by the court. LADIES, LADIES, LADIES......why put your family through this when it can easily be avoided.

There are two major problems with this. First, who will the judge appoint for this position? The answer is whoever goes in front of the judge first and petitions for the position. The judge will not know anything about the incapacitated individual or the dynamics of the family, and will ultimately appoint a person of their own choosing. Often, judges do not choose the person that the incapacitated person would have chosen for the position.

In some cases, the judge's choice will lead to fights and unrest within the family.

The second problem is that the court and the person chosen by the court to handle the financial affairs will remain involved for the entire duration of the person's incapacitation. Family members will have to report to the court with regard to how the money is being spent, and the court will dictate how the money can and cannot be used. Most of us have a trusted family member who we could choose to help us during a time of incapacity, and would not want them to be under such scrutiny.

The financial power of attorney document is simple to put in place, and definitely one of the most important components of an estate plan. In its absence, needless frustration and expenses will take its place.

☐ Health care power of attorney (also called a health care proxy). Every lady out there needs to have a health care power of attorney in place. This document allows a person to choose whom they would like to make medical decisions for them in the event that they are unable to do so themselves.

As ladies, we are used to being the person that everyone else relies on to take care of them. But we, as women, will face a time when we need help from others.

If a woman does not proactively choose someone to make important medical decisions for her, then a judge will do it instead, and the person the judge chooses may or may not even be a family member. Once appointed, this person will again be under the scrutiny of the court.

Every mother who is reading this book needs to make sure that their adult child has a health care power of attorney in place. Once a child reaches the age of 18, they are legally adults, which means their parents will be unable to obtain their medical information or make medical decisions for them.

☐ HIPAA (Health Insurance Portability and Accountability Act). What the heck is HIPAA? Anyone who has ever visited a doctor's office or hospital has most likely been asked to sign a HIPAA form (although few people know why they have to sign it, and even fewer people actually read it first).

By signing a HIPAA authorization form, a person gives their doctors and medical personnel the authority to share their medical information with the people whom they've selected. If a person does not have the capacity to complete a HIPAA form when they enter the hospital, for example due to a brain injury or unconsciousness, then their loved ones may be unable to receive any information about their health status.

This can be prevented by including a HIPAA authorization in your estate plan, which is something every estate planning attorney should encourage their clients to do. Just imagine getting in a car accident and knowing that your family members can't call the hospital and get an update regarding your medical condition. Surely, not many people would want that.

A HIPAA authorization form completed in advance as part of your estate plan is the best way to ensure that loved ones can always receive important medical updates, which is especially valuable when it comes to matters of life and death. There is no doubt this will create peace of mind for everyone.

☐ Living will (advance directive). A living will or advance directive deals with end-of-life decisions. What types of end-of-life treatments should or should not be given? Should life support be allowed, and if so, for how long? Should family members be able to decide to remove life support if the circumstances warrant that?

These are very personal questions that some women feel very strongly about. Putting one's wishes in writing with the use of a living will is a way of communicating one's desires to future health care professionals and family members.

It should be noted that in some states, a person's living will is legally valid and enforceable, while in other states, health professionals may be under no legal authority to honor it.

☐ Wills (Last Will and Testament). Why does every lady need one? Well, who wants the state in which they live to decide where all their assets will go when they die? A will acts as a set of instructions for what an individual wants to have happen to their assets when they pass away. In this document, a person can also name who they want to assume control of their affairs after they pass away.

In order for a will to be valid, it must be properly executed under the laws of the state where the individual lives when they executed the will. It is important to keep in mind that a will only controls assets that are titled in the name of the creator of the will at the time of their death. This means that a will does not control assets that are governed by beneficiary designations, such as life insurance and retirement funds, nor does it control assets that are titled in joint ownership with rights of survivorship (where, when one co-owner dies, the other co-owner becomes the sole owner by operation of law).

Men and women alike tend to think that by putting a will in place, their family members will not have to go through probate. However, a will is actually a guarantee that the assets will have to go through the probate process. This is because a will simply provides instructions to the judge about what the deceased person wanted to have happen with their assets; only a probate judge can change assets from the deceased person's name to the name(s) of their beneficiaries.

☐   Wills and minor children. Women who have minor children or grandchildren should know that having a will in place means having the ability to name a guardian to take care of those minor children or grandchildren in the event that they (and the other legal parent) are unable to. This can be done by simply naming a guardian and/or a conservator in the will. Most of us like to think of this as an unlikely event, but as we all know, life happens when we least expect it; having a plan in place for the children's well-being is a must.

What's Probate? (Sounds Scary, and It Can Be)

Regardless of whether someone has a will, their family will have to go through probate (but not for assets in a trust … and we'll get to that ☺).

The purpose of probate is to change ownership of an asset from the name of the deceased to the name of the beneficiary. The will simply acts as a set of instructions to the probate judge, and only the judge can sign off on the changing of ownership of assets after someone has passed away.

Probate involves the court deciding who will manage the deceased person's affairs now that they have passed, and who the beneficiaries will be. I am positive every strong lady does NOT want to leave such decisions in the hands of a stranger who knows nothing about them or their family.

Probate is also an expensive and time-consuming process. On average, it will take family members two to three times as long to probate their loved one's estate than it would have taken for the deceased person to create an estate plan that ensures an avoidance of probate. On top of that, probate and court fees alone amounted to over $1.5 billion last year (that's a lot of pocketbooks and shoes). And if a woman owns property in multiple states (e.g., a home in

Boston, Massachusetts and a home in Jupiter, Florida), then her family will have to open a probate in each state, doubling the expense.

Most ladies want their children and loved ones to have immediate access to the property and/or money they leave to them. When family members are forced through the probate process, it will be over a year before they can enjoy their benefits. Often the probate process will take much longer depending on the statutory requirements of your state, and how efficient or should I say inefficient the probate courts are. Imagine passing away and knowing that your children can't access the money you left them or, in some cases, even sell your house until more than a year has passed.

Lastly, not many people realize that probate is a very public process; once a probate case is opened, anyone can find out which assets were left to whom. This can not only cause a lot of turmoil within families, but also give people an opportunity to try to take advantage of the beneficiaries.

Trusts

Who are the parties in a trust? Ladies, Ladies, Ladies ... There are only three parties to a trust, and that's all you need to know:

1) Trustor: This refers to the person who created the trust and put their assets into it (think "creator").

2) Trustee: This is the person whom the creator of the trust chooses to have manage all of the assets in the trust (think "manager").

3) Beneficiaries: These are the lucky people who get to benefit from all of the assets in the trust (think "lucky people").

How Trusts Work

Trust-based estate plans are being implemented more and more by all of the ladies out there, whether they are single, divorced, widowed, or married. There are very good reasons for this, which I'll get into.

A trust is simply a contract, just like the contract a consumer has with their cell phone or cable company. In a contract, the rights and responsibilities of the parties involved are clearly defined, and in a trust, the creator gets to define all of the responsibilities of everyone involved (e.g., who will manage their affairs in the event of incapacitation or death, to whom the monies and other assets will go, etc.)—WITHOUT having the courts involved. Since a trust is a contract, it is governed by contract law, so there is no need for a judge to be involved.

Most women want to make it as easy as possible for their family and children after they pass away, and they don't want their family to have to go through the probate process in order to inherit. This is why most women choose to set up a trust while they are alive: they want to make sure that they protect their loved ones from unnecessary risks and expenses.

One of the most powerful benefits of a trust is that, unlike a will, a trust doesn't have to die with the person. In other words, assets can stay in the trust and be managed by the selected trustee until the beneficiaries reach the age(s) at which the creator of the trust wants them to receive their inheritance.

For all of us moms, we know that no matter what we do as parents, none of our children turn out the same ... and oh, what different personalities they have! One child may be introverted and the other extroverted; one book smart and the other good with their hands or amazingly creative; one financially responsible and the other not.

The creator of a trust has the ability to leave each child their inheritance in such a way as to specifically address that child's individual and unique concerns, and protect their inheritance from certain life events that they might one day encounter, such as divorce, creditor issues, and/or just the fallout from poor decision making.

There are different types of trusts that are used in estate planning, but for our purposes here, I am telling all you ladies to focus on the most common type of trust: the revocable trust (also called a revocable living trust). A revocable trust is such an amazing estate planning tool; it allows a person to manage all of their assets the same way they always have (e.g., they can buy, sell, or trade them), and there are no negative tax implications or any reason to file taxes any differently during the creator's lifetime. Last but perhaps most importantly, a revocable trust ensures that the creator's loved ones will not have to deal with the courts. Amazing!

CHAPTER 3

EVERY WOMAN IS UNIQUE — JUST LIKE HER ESTATE PLAN SHOULD BE

Estate plans should fit like a wardrobe — perfectly.

Estate planning is definitely not a one-size-fits-all kind of deal. Every family has unique dynamics and circumstances that must be considered and examined when preparing an estate plan. As our lives evolve, so too do our needs and goals, which means an estate plan will change over time.

But how exactly do estate planning needs differ from one woman to the next? To answer this question, let's start by considering the general life stages of all ladies, and how they impact estate planning.

Twenty and Untouchable

Women in their twenties are really just starting out in life. They're typically focused on getting through the day, and taking steps to establish a career and make more money.

At this stage of life, most women aren't really thinking about what would happen if they were to become incapacitated or die, and we all know that people in their youth never think that these things will happen to them anyway. But the reality is that these things do happen, and when they do, it's a legal and emotional nightmare for the family. This is why it's so important for everyone to have some estate planning documents in place—even people who are only in their twenties.

Thirty and Thriving

When women transition into their thirties, they become focused on their careers and/or their families. For some ladies, career growth is their sole focus, and they put the majority of their time toward climbing the ladder of success in order to reach their personal goals. For other ladies, their attention and focus may be split between climbing the ladder and looking to start and grow a family.

As women begin to increase their wealth and have children, their need for an estate plan comes to the forefront. And for mothers, concerns regarding their children should compel them to immediately address some estate planning needs.

So … why isn't this always the case? As a young mother, I recall my own concerns regarding my children, such as what would happen to them if their father and I passed away. Many women will ask themselves this question or perhaps voice their concerns privately to their loved ones about who they would (and would not) want to care for their children in the event that a tragedy or terminal illness arises.

This is the time when women must answer some key, potentially life-changing questions:

Who will be the guardian for my children?

Can I really trust this person to make life decisions for my children?

Who do I trust to handle the finances I am leaving behind for my children?

Ladies, you work hard to build a career and family, so why would you leave these important decisions to a judge? By neglecting to plan, that is exactly what you are doing, and the judge may not choose the person(s) that you would have chosen. Are you okay with this?

Forty and Fabulous

Ladies in their forties begin to look at life differently; they've matured a bit, or life has matured them. Perhaps they are in a loving marriage with children, or perhaps their marriage has failed and they suddenly find themselves on a whole new journey in life. Maybe they're single and have never married and they're happy with that, or maybe they are truly seeking their soulmate.

Either way, it's during the forties that a woman's estate planning priorities become more and more important, especially as they start to realize that they won't live forever, and want to pass on their assets to their loved ones — the ones they've shared their love and laughter with for so many years.

Some women, by the time they are in their fabulous forties, have already been working to build their retirement fund, while others are just starting the process. Regardless, an estate plan is needed.

Fifty and Free

Ladies in their fifties begin to experience a new sense of freedom. Woohoo! Perhaps their children are grown and gone (or at least almost out of the nest), and there is more free time to be had; it's a time for travel, the rebirth of social activities, and hobbies.

At this age, women have usually experienced the passing of friends and/or family members (whether young or old), and the need to have an effective estate plan in place has either been addressed or is becoming alarmingly important. They begin to really acknowledge that they are aging, and face the thought that anything can happen to them or a loved one. Life's lessons have taught them that life and time are both precious and fleeting.

Legacy Years

In the legacy years, women are finally approaching the second half of their lives and realize that they have fewer years ahead of them than there are behind them. They have matured not only in their looks, but in their minds, and they have come to realize that they (and everyone else) will die at some point; the only question is whether they will face incapacity before that happens.

Many women at this age have watched their grandparents and parents get older, and along the way, learned many lessons they would have never imagined. There is so much dignity and wisdom that comes with age. At this stage in life, estate planning is a must in order to protect loved ones — and that includes making sure their estate plan is up to date.

We all want to do what we can to ensure that our loved ones are protected when we are no longer able to protect them ourselves. But the word 'protect' can mean different things to different people. For some, it means making sure things are as easy as possible for their loved ones; for others, it means making sure their loved one's inheritance doesn't get lost through a divorce, or because of creditor issues. In some cases, protecting a loved one means protecting them from their own poor choices (e.g., addiction, poor spending habits, or perhaps not the best choices in life partners).

Every lady has heard or experienced a horror story or two about the nightmares that can ensue after a loved one has passed away. As women—especially in our legacy years—we will recall different nightmare scenarios and acknowledge that we definitely don't want our family to experience anything even remotely similar.

Most (if not all) of us will worry about the impact the government will have on the monies we plan to leave to our loved ones. We don't want the government (instead of our loved ones) to get any extra money in taxes, especially if it can be avoided with proper estate planning.

Thoughts of how our families would be impacted by our having a stroke or developing a debilitating disease, such as Alzheimer's, will weigh heavily on our minds during this time. And we know we definitely don't want to go into a nursing home — NO, NO, NO, not me! Our money is supposed to go to our loved ones, not nursing homes, but we also need to do what we can to avoid being a burden to our families.

It is apparent — given these changes in our thought processes as we age and mature — that different phases of our lives require different estate planning strategies to address the concerns we have. As life changes, our estate plan documents and strategies may need to change too.

But age certainly isn't the only factor that may influence the need for changes to an estate plan: a change in other demographics will facilitate a need to update an estate plan as well, and women may transition to and from various demographic stages throughout life (e.g., from single to divorced, from mother to grandmother, to business buyer to business seller). All phases will result in a need to re-evaluate the unique circumstances of life at that particular point along the journey.

Let's explore the demographics:

☐ Single women. Whether single by choice or by circumstance, estate planning can go a long way toward ensuring that a single woman has peace of mind, both about her own care and her estate.

For single women with no children, the estate planning process can seem daunting. Who can they trust to handle their finances and take care of them (and perhaps care for their loved ones as well)? Who should benefit from their assets when they die?

It is important for single women to speak with an attorney who really listens to their thoughts and concerns, and who will guide them through some difficult decisions they need to make regarding their affairs.

☐ Married Women. Married women definitely need to plan. If she has a traditional family, (two parents whom are married, with the same biological or adopted children) she will want a plan in place that provides for her spouse, and that protects her money in the event that she becomes incapacitated and needs to be admitted to a nursing home. Just imagine working your whole life to accumulate monies to leave to your children, and suddenly you have to go to a nursing home and spend all of that money on your own care. (In Massachusetts and New Hampshire, monthly nursing expenses are around $15,000 a month.)

There are also estate planning strategies that ensure that some or all of the assets will be preserved in the event that a woman's spouse becomes incapacitated and/or needs nursing home care. Failing to plan in the event of an incapacity can leave a woman without the ability to not only protect her assets, but to make financial and medical decisions regarding her spouse. Just imagine having to go to court to receive approval by a judge in order to access your spouse's bank accounts and thereby survive and pay the bills. This could be devasting—both financially and emotionally—for a family.

☐ Divorced women. For newly divorced women, it is imperative that they meet with their estate planning attorney. Women don't always realize that they may have named their ex-spouse as the beneficiary of their bank account, life insurance policies, and/or retirement accounts. Unless there is a court order stating the ex-spouse must be the beneficiary of these accounts, the divorced woman will want to change this designation as soon as possible.

Further, if the woman completed any estate planning documents prior to the divorce, then she will want to update those documents as soon as the divorced is finalized. This could prevent some very serious problems, such as the ex-spouse maintaining the authority to handle the woman's affairs or receive all of her assets after she passes.

It's not uncommon for spouses to list each other as the person who can make medical and financial decisions for them, which is something that should be changed after a divorce. In most states, a divorce itself will nullify such designations, but it's best to make sure of this. This is especially true since a medical provider might not be aware of the divorce, and therefore might not think twice about listening to and exchanging medical information with the ex-spouse.

If a divorced woman has adult children, she may want to designate one of them to make financial and medical decisions for her, as well as handle her affairs once she passes away. She will also want to make sure that if she wants her children to be the sole beneficiaries of her estate, her estate planning documents reflect this.

☐ Widowed women. A newly-widowed woman usually needs to work with an estate planning attorney, but often doesn't realize it. Grieving the loss of her spouse and feeling overwhelmed, she may let a long time pass before even thinking about contacting an estate planning attorney. This can be extremely dangerous. If there are no estate planning documents in place, then state law will govern exactly what the surviving spouse is entitled to, and who will receive which assets.

People often wrongly assume that when their spouse passes away, they will inherit everything, so they fail to plan. The truth is that the state statute will decide, and depending on the state, a surviving spouse may or may not be the sole beneficiary. Statutes take into consideration the family dynamics, such as separate and/or joint children who may be alive when the first spouse passes away.

Good intentions are only as good as the paper they are written on. If a woman truly wants to have a say about where her assets will go when she passes away, then a written, legal estate plan is necessary.

There may be many things that a woman needs to be aware of prior to her spouse passing, such as the location of important documents and passwords, and knowledge of her spouse's assets and jointly-owned assets. Having access to this type of information will be imperative to dealing with the estate after the death of a spouse. Most people wouldn't even know how to begin the process, but there are professionals available to help people through this. We offer a downloadable Ladies Legacies workbook to help all of you organize this information at www.kellylongtinlaw.com

The death of a spouse can be extremely traumatizing but failing to call an estate planning attorney as soon as possible can make dealing with the estate even more complicated and troublesome.

☐ Re-married women. If a woman has recently tied the knot, then a congratulations is in order! Now is the time to create an estate plan if there isn't already one, or review the existing plan. There should be a conversation about how the assets belonging to each spouse and within the marriage will be handled.

For instance, some couples like to keep their assets separate (as they did prior to the marriage), while others will want to combine their assets after marriage. Other couples find a happy medium where some assets are separate and some are joint. Regardless of the choice, each spouse will need their own estate plan that addresses who will have the authority to make financial and medical decisions on their behalf.

If trusts are determined to be a proper estate planning strategy, then the spouses can choose to each have their own separate trust, or a joint trust together.

The trust strategy that makes sense for a given circumstance will depend on a number of factors, such as family dynamics and members, assets and allocation, the law regarding federal and state estate taxes, and the overall goals of the family.

☐ Women in a blended family. For any woman who is considered to be part of a blended family — whether after a first or subsequent marriage — an effective estate plan in place is an absolute must. A "blended family" is a family that includes at least one child where only one of the spouses is the parent. Estate planning for blended families adds a level of complexity that does not exist in traditional families, where any and all children come from the spouses.

In a blended family situation, the first thing a woman should ask herself is what she wants to have happen when she dies. Conversations about what will happen when one spouse dies and where the assets will go after both spouses die can be very difficult, which is why people often avoid having them at all — or at least not until they really have to. That's when couples usually find themselves sitting in front of an estate planning attorney.

The first thing that should be determined between spouses is whether their objectives are in alignment. If they are, then working together to put a joint plan in place might make sense; if they are not, then both spouses may need their own estate planning attorneys to handle their individual plans.

A married woman in a blended family should also consider how she plans to provide for her spouse in the event that she passes away first. Is her goal to provide 100% of her assets to her surviving spouse, or to leave her spouse a portion of her assets but to primarily care for her children? What if the house is just in her name and she wants to leave it to her kids? Does she want to make sure that her surviving spouse would have a place to live for the rest of their life, or for a fixed amount of time?

Depending on the relationship and the finances, a woman may want her spouse to have free reign over the finances when she passes, or may want to limit her spouse's control over the finances to ensure that her children will inherit what she intends for them to inherit.

If a woman and her spouse in a blended family have minor children, then they will need to have a conversation about who will care for them if she passes away and they are still minors. Would it be her spouse or the children's natural parent? Under the law, the natural parent would have precedence, but what if the woman and her spouse have raised the children for the majority of their lives? Under such circumstances, it would be in the best interests of the children for the woman's surviving spouse to maintain a relationship with them.

The death of a parent is extremely traumatizing at such a young age, and having stability and support will be extremely important. Having this conversation with the child and the people involved ahead of time can be helpful in designing a plan that will best benefit the children in their time of need.

☐ Unmarried with a long-term partner. How does estate planning change if a woman has decided not to marry her long-term partner? With more and more women deciding not to marry, this is a topic that needs to be addressed. If a woman is in a committed long- term relationship, chances are that she will want that person to be an integral part of life, even after she passes away; it's critical to have estate planning documents in place to ensure that this happens.

Imagine, for instance, that a woman's partner suddenly becomes ill and is in the hospital, and the medical professionals are looking for someone to make medical decisions for him/her. Or perhaps it is the woman who has suffered a medical crisis, and the medical professionals are looking for someone to make medical decisions for her. If there is no health care power of attorney in place naming the long-term partner as the person who should make medical decisions, then a family member (instead of the long-term partner) might step into this role.

Far too many times, I have seen this happen: a partner in a long-term relationship experiences an unexpected tragedy, and the person they most care about is unable to have any say in important life (or death) decisions. Instead, the long-term partner may be excluded from the decision-making process and might not even be informed as to what is going on—a terrible feeling.

It is equally important to have a financial power of attorney in place in the event that one partner in a long-term relationship becomes incapacitated or unable to manage their finances. Chances are good that the couple will share some financial burdens, whether it is paying for property together, or just handling the household bills. If one partner suddenly becomes incapacitated, the other partner may find themselves without the legal authority to access their partner's financial accounts.

Another issue that seems so apparent but often goes unrealized is that a partner in a long-term relationship may want to leave their assets to their partner after they pass. Without an estate plan that dictates this, and unless the couple owned property jointly with rights of survivorship, the state statute will govern who is going to be the beneficiary of the decedent's estate.

Imagine spending the better part of your life building a future with your loved one, only to find out the hard way that without a will or a trust in place stating who should inherit the assets, the surviving partner may end up with nothing!

☐ Mothers. Okay, Momma Bears, we all know how protective we can be of our children. One of the best ways to protect them is by setting up a proper estate plan and making it as easy as possible for them after we pass away or become incapacitated, which means making sure that they will not have to be subjected to court involvement. It can also mean ensuring that our wishes are made clear in order to limit fighting amongst the kids.

Through the right estate plan, mothers can consider how they want to leave their inheritance to their beneficiaries. For example, if one of her children is facing an impending divorce, she will want to ensure that their inheritance does not get divided or lost through the divorce process. The same protection strategies can be used against a beneficiary's pending lawsuit or pattern of poor decision making.

As mothers, we are always trying to protect our children as they navigate through life, so why wouldn't we protect them when we are no longer alive to do so? It has always been interesting to me that people are so passionate about caring for their children and families while they are able to, but when they have the opportunity to make their children's lives easier and protect them after they've passed away, they fail to act on it.

☐ Lady Bosses. More and more women are starting small businesses and thriving, but business succession planning is not something that most female business owners have considered. Some women assume that their business will have no value once they are gone, but that is not always true. Proactively determining the value of a business and the possibility of a sale upon death will ease the burden that falls on the woman's family. Some women want to pass on their business to their children, which can be done in a timely, peaceful, and cost-effective manner with the right estate plan.

Protecting business interests, now and in the future. Depending on whether a business is a sole proprietorship, partnership, LLC, or corporation, the lady business owner will need to ensure that her interests are conveyed clearly after she passes away. This is possible with a proper estate plan that includes a plan for business succession or the passing of the business assets through the estate plan, without the need for probate.

When a business is involved, I like to use trust-based planning, because by implementing trusts, we can assign the interests from the business to the trust, and dictate where and how those assets will be distributed after the owner passes away.

CHAPTER 4

ESTATE PLANNING EVASION (THE MOST COMMON EXCUSES)

Over 54% of women in the United States do not have a will or any estate planning documents in place.

I believe the biggest reason women don't plan is lack of education about the importance of estate planning. It is not easy to learn or speak about the possibility that one may, at some point in time, lose their independence and ability to take care of themselves. It is even more difficult to discuss the certainty of death.

Although lack of education is a major factor for woman failing to plan, other factors have an influence on women as well:

☐ Lack of confidence about finances. Too many women don't plan their estate because they do not feel confident about their finances. Sometimes this lack of confidence comes from a lack of education, but oftentimes, it is a derivative of a bad experience they had with a condescending or patronizing advisor who left them feeling insecure about money matters.

It is not uncommon for my female clients to relay to me an experience they had with an advisor, during which they were made to feel inadequate. In a world where the advisor's job is to advise, this seems like a counterintuitive approach for a professional to take.

Historically, men have been brought into the financial planning folds early in life. As little boys, they are taught how to make money, how to save it, how to spend it, and how to invest it. Thinking back to their childhood, many women realize that these conversations were never had with them. Sometimes they occurred later in life, and most often by adults outside the family, but oftentimes these conversations were never had at all.

The irony of this is that women will predominately be left behind to manage their family's wealth, and the wealth of our country. Despite progress in granting women more rights, cultural attitudes about money and finance have been slow to shift, which continues to contribute to this ongoing lack of confidence felt by women.

☐ The feeling that no one is listening. Common feedback from female clients is that they do not feel like their concerns are being heard. It is definitely difficult for a person to want to talk about something that is important to them when they feel like no one is listening. Sometimes women feel like this due to the nature of their relationship, such as their spouse being predominantly in control of the decisions. Other times, it may be the result of an overbearing child or other family member, who undoubtedly means well, but who has asserted themselves in a way that makes the female feel insignificant and powerless.

☐ Gender Norms. As a society, we have come a long way from Adam and Eve and the Flintstones, but gender norm ideas still exist and impact the behaviors of men and women. Historically, women were raised to be nurturing, and were taught to manage familial relationships and to take care of the house, the cooking, and the children. Men, on the other hand, were raised to be assertive, to make money for the household, and to be responsible for financial and legal matters.

Although many of the traditional biases of males and females are outdated and not consciously thought about, they do tend to trickle into our lives as a result of our upbringings. What has not changed significantly is that women are still the primary caretakers and the emotional backbone of their families.

It is imperative that women begin to take a more active role when it comes to learning about and managing their finances, as this will help them build the confidence necessary to create a solid and reliable plan for the future.

☐ Too young to worry about it. Some women ask if they are too young to put an estate plan in place. I do not believe anyone is ever too young to put an estate plan in place. Why? Because no one has a crystal ball; no one knows what their future holds, or when or how they might become incapacitated or die.

Young women with young children must put a plan in place in order to choose who they would want to care for their children in the event that they can no longer do it themselves—and this includes handling financial matters for any minor children they leave behind.

In the absence of a legal plan, the courts will choose who they believe to be the best candidate for these roles. If a family member is available and interested in filling these roles, the courts will usually choose them. However, the courts can and do appoint complete strangers to these roles as well. Just the thought of a complete stranger overseeing the well-being of a child who has just lost their mom should be the prompt one needs to get their estate plan in place.

☐ Too expensive. It is my belief that women only feel like it may be too expensive to put an estate plan in place if they do not truly understand the value of a proper estate plan and how effective it can be in addressing a woman's main estate planning concerns. A good estate plan can ensure that a particular person of the woman's choosing makes medical and financial decisions on her behalf, should she become unable to make these types of decisions herself. It can also help ensure a smooth transition of the woman's assets to her loved ones upon her death, help maintain the relationships in the family, and avoid the costs of court involvement. These are priceless benefits. By investing in a proper estate plan, a woman can rest assured knowing that she has saved her loved ones' time, money, and aggravation.

☐ The assumption that it's unnecessary. Some women feel as if they do not need to put an estate plan in place. This is especially true among single women who do not yet have a family. However, anyone who wants to have a say about what should happen if they were to become incapacitated or pass away should have an estate plan.

A married woman may assume that as long as her spouse has a will or trust, she doesn't need one. Or, she might simply assume that she does not have sufficient assets in her own name to warrant making an estate plan. Such assumptions can be very costly because they ignore the probability that the wife will survive her spouse, and therefore likely receive the bulk of her spouse's estate (which might be sizable). It also ignores the possibility that the wife will inherit from her parents.

Depending on the generation, a woman might think that if the property is held primarily in the name of her husband, then she does not need to partake in estate planning. Other times, women believe that owning property jointly or having beneficiaries on their accounts means that they do not need to put an estate plan in place. If jointly-held assets are held as joint tenants with rights of survivorship, then when one owner dies, the property will automatically be owned by the other owner. But what happens once that spouse (the woman) becomes the only remaining owner of the property? Such property would have to be dealt with in probate after the woman passes away. This can be avoided by properly planning your estate.

IRAs, life insurance policies, and some bank accounts will automatically transfer to the beneficiaries listed on those accounts. The key is to make sure that the people listed as beneficiaries should still be listed as such. If one or more of the listed beneficiaries is a minor, then an estate planning attorney should be consulted so that there is no misunderstanding in terms of whether and to what degree the courts might have to be involved.

CHAPTER 5

A TRUSTED ESTATE PLAN MEANS A TRUSTED ESTATE PLANNING ATTORNEY

"Those who represent themselves have fools for clients."

As an estate planning attorney, my philosophy has always been to focus on building and growing relationships with my clients and their families. I like to meet with my clients on an annual basis to see what's been going on in their lives, and to review their estate planning strategy in light of any important changes.

For some people, life tends to stay at the status quo, but for others, a single year can be full of many significant changes. Many of my clients do not understand how an event in their lives can affect their estate plan; it is my job to stay "in the know" and advise them of any estate plan revisions that might be necessary or helpful.

Over time, friendships, family dynamics, and feelings change. A once close and trusted family friend could drift away, move to a different country, or even pass away, which might warrant a change to an existing estate plan. Many people reach out to me after having gone years or even decades without speaking to their estate planning attorney, and as a result, they come to me with outdated estate planning documents that no longer align with their goals and desires. It's critical to ensure that any existing plan accurately reflects the ongoing wishes of its creator.

Not All Estate Plans Are Created Equal

When it comes to creating an estate plan that will effectively protect and provide for a woman's family when they are no longer able to themselves, experience definitely matters. It amazes me that people will expose their loved ones to the very things they are trying to protect them from — and all because they do not work with a qualified estate planning attorney.

When people rely on themselves to create an estate plan or they bargain shop in this area, all they are doing is giving themselves a false sense of security. They think they can confidently cross off estate planning from their list, but can they? Can they really be sure that the will or trust they created is even valid under state law? The validity of these documents depends on whether they were drafted correctly, but also on whether the requirements specifically governed by state law were properly followed and implemented.

DIY and Online Documents — I Think I Can Do This All by Myself ☺

Ladies, listen to me! CREATING A WILL OR A TRUST, OR ANY ESTATE PLANNING DOCUMENT ONLINE is a major mistake. But the truth is that women don't always realize this until a death or an incapacity has already occurred and the estate plan they created online does not work as they thought it would.

Estate planning laws are governed by each and every state. Online forms for the creation of a will may have a drop-down menu where the user can choose their state, but this doesn't mean that those forms will be properly drafted under the laws of that state (and oftentimes they are not).

Further, a will is unlikely to be the only estate planning document a person needs. I say this with the utmost respect, but a person who is not a lawyer has not received legal education or legal training and is unlikely to know which documents they need to implement and how to implement them in order to best protect their family in the present and in the future.

Most people in the world understand the basics of a will, but few understand what's required in order to have a valid and enforceable will. Not only do people have to worry about the proper execution of a will, trust, and other estate planning documents, but also about the clauses within them; most people don't understand these clauses, and/or assume they are standard and that their inclusion or exclusion will not really affect the overall estate plan.

If a DIY will or trust is not valid, then the person(s) to whom the creator intended to leave their assets could end up with nothing, and instead, the assets will go to the individual's heirs specified under state law (and these might be the very last people the individual would have wanted to receive all of their hard-earned assets).

A proper estate plan will address not only what happens when the individual passes away, but also what happens if they become incapacitated. It will address the minimization of estate taxes, and allow the creator of the estate plan to protect their assets. Accomplishing all of this accurately online, through DIY methods, and/or without the assistance of the right estate planning attorney is extremely unlikely.

Trying to use an online service or a DIY strategy to conquer the complexities of estate planning could mean failing to protect loves ones and failing to meet any estate planning objectives in the long run.

When a Bad Plan Is Worse Than No Plan at All

A poorly-constructed estate plan can in some cases be worse than having no plan at all. For example, let's assume someone wants to make sure that when they pass away, their assets are inherited by their children. Now let's assume that this person was to mistakenly believe that this would happen as long as they make their spouse the primary beneficiary of their accounts and assets, and list their children as the contingent or subsequent beneficiaries if the spouse passes away. Most people would assume, understandably, that their assets would first go to their spouse, and then to their children once their spouse passes away.

But will this actually happen? Maybe ... or maybe NOT. The truth is that when someone leaves all of their estate to their spouse before passing away, their spouse can do anything they want with those assets — including taking it all and leaving the children with nothing. This can be avoided with the implementation of a proper estate plan that addresses these concerns and makes sure that no one is accidentally disinherited.

Poorly-constructed estate plans commonly lead to overpayment of taxes (with money that would have been better spent by the surviving family members) and expensive, needless court processes and legal battles (again, money better spent by the surviving family members).

An experienced estate planning attorney can help people understand how various potential situations and contingencies could impact their estate plan and lead to unintended consequences that contradict the desired estate planning outcomes.

Not All Estate Planning Attorneys Are Created Equal

While I love my fellow colleagues greatly, not every attorney is created equal. There, I said it. Part of my personality is being honest and upfront with people so here goes: an EXPERIENCED ESTATE PLANNING ATTORNEY can make all the difference in the world for a family.

Law school students study six to seven areas of law, and it would be nearly impossible to actively practice in all these areas and be great in any one of them. And when it comes to estate planning, which is such a vast area of law, I can't even imagine having to truly know all of the ins and outs of it in addition to other areas of law. "Jill of all trades, but master of none" is what comes to mind — which isn't what anyone needs when it comes to estate planning.

The medical field has become very specialized, and for good reason: there are just too many things for a person to focus on in any one area, and the benefit of having doctors focus on one area of medicine as specialists has become clear. Who would want to go to a cardiologist for a broken leg? Sure, the cardiologist could probably determine that the person has a broken leg, but would they be able to implement the right plan for helping that bone heal properly?

Similarly, who would want to go to a general or DUI or divorce attorney when they need an estate plan? Who would feel comfortable putting the most important things in their life—including their legacy and loved ones—in the hands of a part-time practitioner of estate planning? Why would someone who needs an estate plan hire anyone other than an attorney who specializes in estate planning?

Incredible benefits result from attorneys who decide to focus on one area of the law so that they can spend all of their time and energy becoming a true master of it—learning all the ins and outs and thereby achieving the best possible outcomes for their clients.

This is why I focus solely on estate planning, as I always have, and it's why I firmly believe that people should hire an estate planning attorney who focuses primarily or entirely on estate planning. So many pitfalls—from family fallout and negative tax consequences, to nursing home problems and court involvement—can be avoided by hiring a true expert in the field.

Every family presents unique circumstances which need to be considered when creating an effective estate plan. With every client, I start the initial meeting with an in-depth conversation about their family dynamics, assets, and goals — and every truly qualified estate planning attorney should do the same. This is truly the only way that a great estate plan can be created.

Kelly Longtin Law

Estate planning is the only type of law I have ever practiced. I was lucky enough to land a job with an estate planning firm on the day I took the bar exam. Thank God I passed!!!

I have always had a passion for helping others, especially others who can't really help themselves. Having been so positively impacted by the stories told to me as a child by my grandparents, I felt even more compelled to protect them as they aged and were slowly overtaken by fragileness.

Now, I want to do whatever I can to protect other people's grandparents, parents, children, and other loved ones. When meeting with each and every family, my promise is to treat them the same way I would want someone to treat my aging grandparents or parents—with kindness, patience, and honesty.

I am grateful that I possess an amazing skill that helps strangers feel comfortable opening up to and confiding in me, even about their most inner thoughts, secrets, and concerns. I believe that my true, genuine interest in caring for other families as much as I do my own is what has allowed me to be successful in a field of law where what really matters most in life always rises to the top....... Family.

APPENDIX

LADIES LEGACIES™: WORKBOOK AND GUIDE
(You can also download it at
www.kellylongtinlaw.com)

We hope this guide will provide you with a stepping stone to "being in the know" about your finances.

The truth of the matter is that we can't predict the future. We don't know when our time is up, and the same goes for our spouses. Grieving the loss of a loved one can be truly devastating, not to mention highly stressful. By taking the time to talk about this important topic, you can eliminate the financial aspect of your stress.

Complete this little workbook and get on the same page about finances. You're a strong woman; I have complete confidence that you will learn this information in no time. They say that knowledge is power, and this instance is no different.

Once you have your estate plan in place, don't keep it a secret! Tell your children and/or other loved ones about it. Explain the choices you've made so that there are no surprises down the road.

Ultimately, being prepared and knowing your finances is a part of the lasting legacy you'll leave behind.

Don't be afraid to sound your voice. You have created a wonderful foundation and are keyed into the family finances. You can be confident in yourself to take the reins when that time comes.

With knowledge and insight into your finances, you have put yourself on the path to long-term financial stability. But remember, you don't have to be superwoman and do it all. If and when you find yourself in charge of the finances, remember this: you don't have to do it alone. Reach out to a friend or trusted advisor who can support you financially and practically. You will have complete knowledge of your financial picture, and together, you'll be able to navigate this difficult time.

In the meantime, there are things you can do to make things easier on yourself:

• Get an estate plan. Everyone needs an estate plan – no one is too old, too young, too wealthy, or too poor. The sooner the better!

• Keep your estate plan up to date. Life changes; make sure your plan matches your life situation.

• Continue to stay up to date on your finances. Don't let this be a one-time occurrence – keep this information current!

Workbook

Location, Location, Location

Is all of your financial information in one area? Circle one:

Yes   No

If you answered yes, where is it? Is it easily accessible?

_____

_____

If you answered no, where is it? Can it easily be moved to a single location?

_____

_____

If your financial information can all be filed in the same place, make a plan to do that. It will be much easier to find in an emergency. A filing cabinet or a spare desk drawer is a great solution. If possible, reserve it only for your personal financial information.

What about the location of these important documents/items?

Insurance Policies:

_____

Bank/Brokerage Statement:

_____

Stock/Bond Certificates:

_____

Real Estate Deeds:

_____

Safe Deposit Box Keys:

Social Security Numbers:

_____

Birth Certificates:

_____

Marriage Certificates:

_____

Other Important Documents:

_____

_____

_____

Don't forget to tell your loved ones or whoever will need to find these important documents after you pass or become incapacitated where to find all this information.

Remember to consider your online accounts and assets. As the world is trending toward the electronic storage of information, more is focused on digital assets. Keeping track of these accounts as well as passwords and/or security questions can save your loved ones' time and trouble trying to access the information needed.

E-Mail Accounts:

User Name:

_____

Password:

_____

Security Question:

_____

Security Answer:

_____

Social Media Accounts:

Name of Social Media:

_____

User Name: _____

Password: _____

Name of Social Media:

_____

User Name: _____

Password: _____

Name of Social Media:

_____

User Name: _____

Password: _____

Websites/Blogs:

_____

_____

_____

_____

Cloud Storage:

Webpage: _____

User Name: _____

Password:_____

Security Question: _____

Security Answer: _____

Financial Transactions:

Webpage: _____

User Name: _____

Password:_____

Security Question: _____

Security Answer: _____

Webpage: _____

User Name: _____

Password:_____

Security Question: _____

Security Answer: _____

Webpage: _____

User Name: _____

Password:_____

Security Question: _____

Security Answer: _____

Webpage: _____

User Name: _____

Password:_____

Security Question: _____

Security Answer: _____

Remember to include any other online accounts that you may want loved ones to have access to, such as music downloads, photos, writing, gaming, or any online virtual property accounts such as Venmo, Paypal, etc., that may have balances on them.

_____
_____
_____
_____
_____
_____
_____
_____
_____
_____
_____
_____
_____
_____

You have created a great framework for your plan and are closer to answering a very important question about your financial future:

If you were to be on your own, could you sustain your current lifestyle?

By using this financial information and updating your budget regularly you will be in a great position to answer that question.

To keep your budget updated, regularly gather bills and other relevant information (don't forget your online bills) and get on the same page about the details and status of all accounts.

Once you are able to determine the location of all these important documents then you will need to dive deep into the family finances. Answering the following questions will provide a great outline to create or update a plan for your finances.

What are the sources of income for your household? Example: paycheck, social security, pension, rental income, annuity, pensions, etc.

Source   When Received   How Much   How Received

_____

_____

_____

_____

_____

_____

This information will not only be useful to you when preparing your budget and assessing your financial future, but will also assist your loved ones in the event of your incapacity or death.

What are your monthly and annual bills? When are they paid and how are they paid? Example: Online, Phone, Mail or Direct Debit from an account?

Name	Amount	When Paid	How Paid

FINANCIAL INFORMATION:

Bank/Institution: _____

Type of Account: _____

Act#: _____

Account Holder Name:

_____

Bank/Institution:

_____

Type of Account: _____

Act#: _____

Account Holder Name:

_____

Bank/Institution:

_____

Type of Account: _____

Act#: _____

Account Holder Name:

_____

Bank/Institution:

_____

Type of Account: _____

Act#: _____

Account Holder Name:

_____

EMPLOYEE BENEFITS:

Name of Institution:

_____

Act#: _____

Type of Benefit:

_____

_____

Contact Name: _____

Contact Number: _____

Name of Institution:

_____

Act#: _____

Type of Benefit:

_____

Contact Name: _____

Contact Number: _____

OTHER IMPORTANT ACCOUNTS:

_____

_____

_____

_____

_____

_____

_____

My Asset Information

Life Insurance:

Name of Company

_____

Policy #: _____

Amount _____

Current Primary Beneficiary:

_____

Current Contingent
Beneficiary:_____

Life Insurance:

Name of Company

_____

Policy #: _____

Amount _____

Current Primary
Beneficiary:_____

Current Contingent
Beneficiary:_____

Annuity:

Name of Institution_____

Account #: _____

Current Primary Beneficiary:

_____

Current Contingent
Beneficiary:_____

Annuity:

Name of Institution_____

Account #: _____

Current Primary Beneficiary:

_____

Current Contingent
Beneficiary:_____

401K:

Name of Institution _____

Policy#: _____

Amount _____

Current Primary Beneficiary:

_____

Current Contingent
Beneficiary:_____

401K:

Name of Institution _____

Policy#: _____

Amount _____

Current Primary Beneficiary:

_____

Current Contingent
Beneficiary:_____

IRA:

Name of Institution _____

Policy#: _____

Amount _____

Current Primary Beneficiary:

_____

Current Contingent
Beneficiary:_____

IRA:

Name of Institution _____

Policy#: _____

Amount _____

Current Primary Beneficiary:

_____

Current Contingent Beneficiary:

_____

Brokerage/Investment Account:

Name of Institution _____

Account # _____

Contact Info: _____

Brokerage/Investment Account:

Name of Institution _____

Account # _____

Contact Info: _____

Money Market Account:

Name of Institution _____

Account # _____

Value: _____

Money Market Account:

Name of Institution _____

Account # _____

Value: _____

CD Account:

Name of Institution _____

Account # _____

Value: _____

CD Account:

Name of Institution _____

Account # _____

Value: _____

Stocks:

Name of Stock _____

Cert # _____

# of shares_____

Stocks:

Name of Stock _____

Cert # _____

# of shares_____

Stocks:

Name of Stock _____

Cert # _____

# of shares_____

My Family History

Father's Name

_____

Date of Birth   Date of Death

_____

Place of Birth

_____

Cause of Death

_____

Place of Burial

_____

Siblings Names:

_____

_____

_____

Mother's Maiden Name   *Married Name*

_____

_____

Date of Birth   Date of Death

_____

_____

Place of Birth

_____

_____

Cause of Death

_____

_____

Place of Burial

_____

_____

Siblings Names:

_____

_____

_____

My Information

My Children

Name: _____

Date of Birth: _____

Name: _____

Date of Birth: _____

Name: _____

Date of Birth: _____

Name: _____

Date of Birth: _____

Name: _____

Date of Birth: _____

Name: _____

Date of Birth: _____

My Grandchildren

Name: _____

Date of Birth: _____

Name: _____

Date of Birth: _____

Name: _____

Date of Birth: _____

Name: _____

Date of Birth: _____

Name: _____

Date of Birth: _____

Name: _____

Date of Birth: _____

Name: _____

Date of Birth: _____

Name: _____

Date of Birth: _____

Name: _____

Date of Birth: _____

Name: _____

Date of Birth: _____

Notify In Case Of Emergency

Name: _____

Phone Number:_____

Relationship _____

Name: _____

Phone Number: _____

Relationship _____

My Legal Documents

My Original Will is located at:

_____

_____

My Original Trust is located at:

_____

_____

My Original Power of Attorney is located at:

_____

_____

My Original Healthcare Power of Attorney is located at:

_____

_____

Attorney/Law Firm Who Prepared Documents:

_____

_____

Attorney Address & Telephone Number:

_____

_____

My Employment Information

Name of Employer:

_____

_____

Address of Employer:

_____

_____

Telephone # of Employer:

_____

Supervisor Name:

_____

Life Insurance Through Employer:

____Yes _____ No

Retirement Account Through Employer:

____Yes _____ No

Pension: ____ Yes ___ No

Any Other Accounts Through Employer:

____ Yes ____ No

If YES, please list description:

_____

INDEX

NOTES